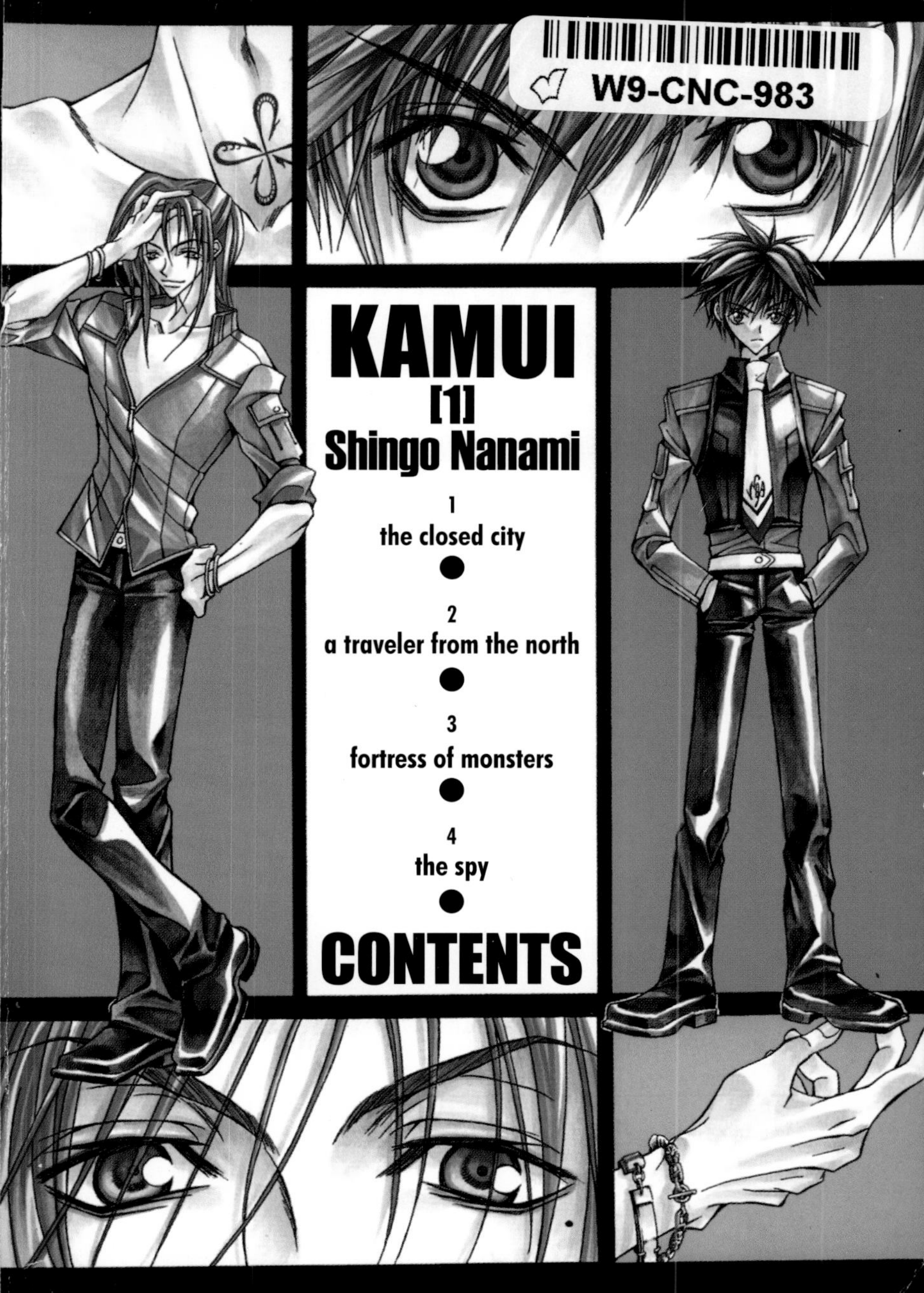

KAMUI

[1]

Shingo Nanami

CONTENTS

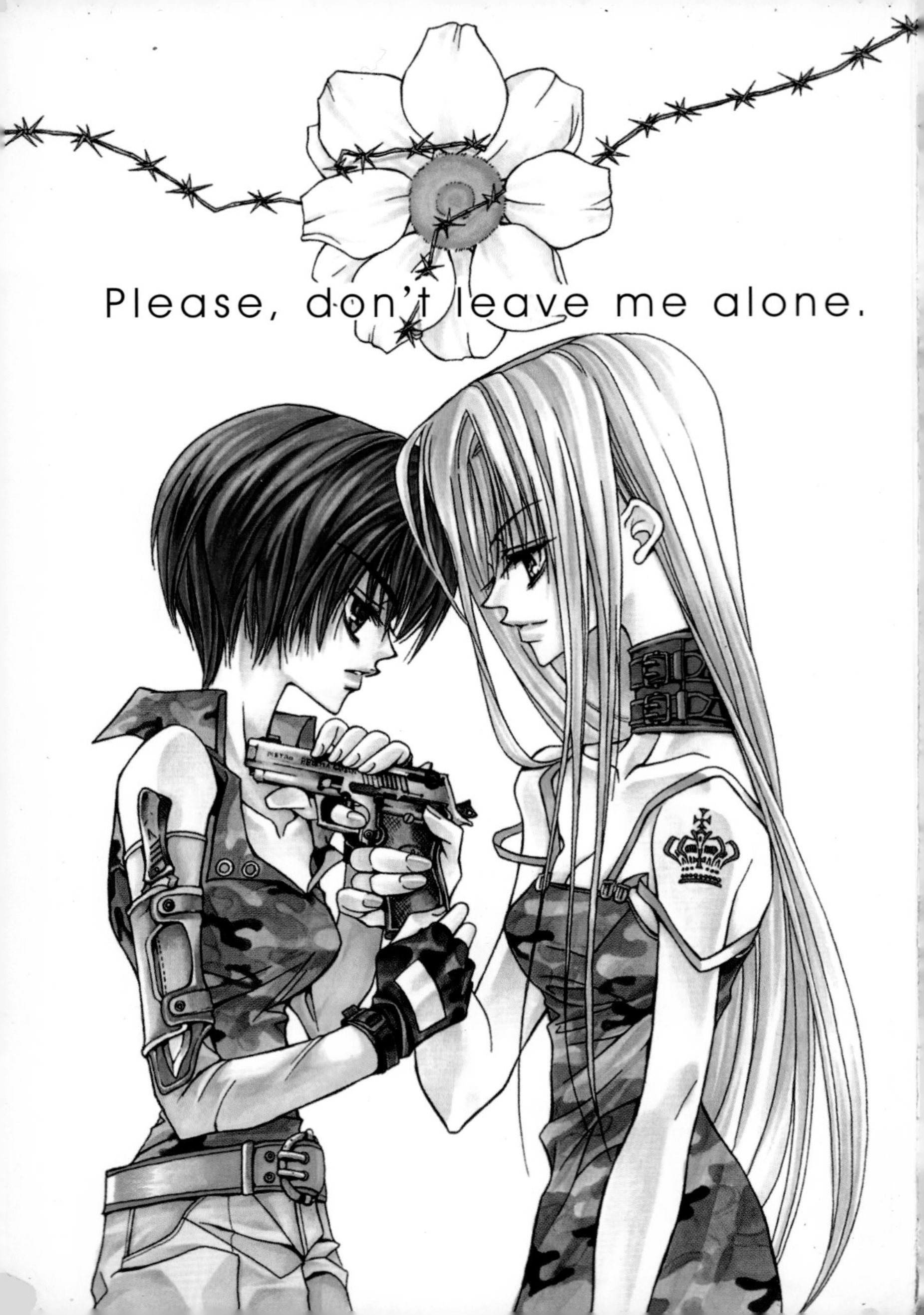
Please, don't leave me alone.

KAMUI
カムイ
1
七海慎吾
Shingo Nanami

KAMUI

BY SHINGO NANAMI

KAMUI Volume 1

English Adaptation Staff
Translation: Satsuki Yamashita
English Adaptation: Elizabeth Hanel
Touch-Up, & Lettering: Fawn "tails" Lau
Cover & Graphic Supervision: Chris McDougall

Editor: Dietrich Seto
Sales Manager: Ardith D. Santiago
Managing Editor: Shizuki Yamashita
Publisher: Kaname Tezuka

Email: editor@broccolibooks.com
Website: www.bro-usa.com

A BROCCOLI BOOKS Manga
Broccoli Books is a division of Broccoli International USA, Inc.
P.O. Box 66078 Los Angeles, CA 90066

ISBN-13: 978-1-5974-1048-9
ISBN-10: 1-5974-1048-9

Published by Broccoli International USA, Inc.
First printing, November 2005

All illustrations by Shingo Nanami.

www.bro-usa.com

10 9 8 7 6 5 4 3 2 1
Printed in the United States

KAMUI

TABLE OF CONTENTS

カムイ CHARACTERS

ATSUMA
A young man who is sent by his village in the north to retrieve the stolen sacred spirit, Okikurumi. Betrayed by someone he once admired, he trusts no one and keeps himself distanced from others. He is infused with the spirit of an ancient sword.

SUMIRE
NOA's second-in-command and Tensho (Commander of the Heaven Division). Bored and lonely, she brings Atsuma into NOA hoping to witness the miracle of which he speaks. She is infused with the power of the wind.

SHUI
Second lieutenant at NOA who takes Atsuma under his wing. An adept cook that likes to take care of others, his voice holds a strange attraction for both Atsuma and Sumire. He is infused with the power of fire.

CHARACTERS カムイ

SHIKI
The top general of NOA. Despite assuming an air of royalty, he is unemotional. He uses NOA as a cage to keep Sumire bound to him.

AIKA
First lieutenant at NOA and Sumire's right-hand woman. She is completely devoted to Sumire and only wishes to be by her side. She appears to be strict and uncaring, which comes from her reluctance to trust anyone but Sumire.

HYDE
Lieutenant general of NOA and holds the number three position behind Sumire. As the Chisho, he is in charge of the Earth Division. Crazy and sadistic, he is obsessed with destruction.

YANAGI
First lieutenant of NOA and Hyde's right-hand man. He is both smart and calculating. Although loyal to Hyde, he keeps in close contact with Shiki.

Chapter
01 the closed city

IN ALL OBJECTS, SPIRITS LIVE.

Long ago, the spirits and mankind lived side by side.
They worked together in mutual cooperation.
Until man forgot the ties that bound them together.
Man awakened to science, and became obsessed with technology.
Cities grew. It seemed as though they would cover the Earth.
Until...

...THERE WERE CONSEQUENCES.

WOOOO
NOT A THING LEFT STANDING.

THOSE BUILDINGS LOOKED INDESTRUCTIBLE.

BUT ALL THAT'S LEFT IS A PILE OF JUNK.

NO MATTER HOW FAST A SOCIETY GROWS...

...IT CAN ALL END IN A MOMENT.

THERE'S NO PRECISE DATA ON THE NUMBER OF CASUALTIES. IT'S AN UNPRECEDENTED NATURAL DISASTER.

THE SECOND GREAT EARTH-QUAKE, KNOWN AS THE GRAND SINKER.

RUSTLE

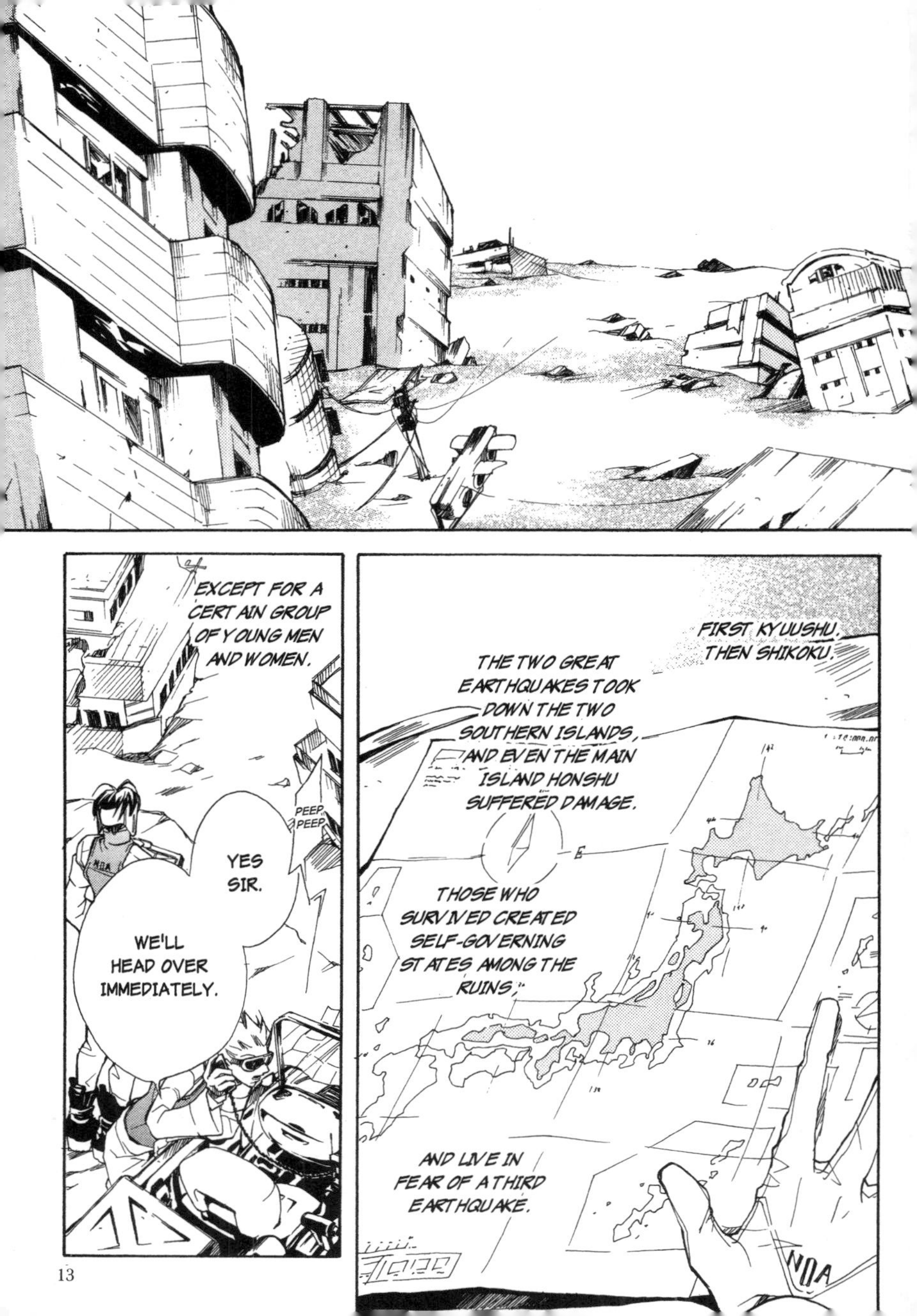

FIRST KYUUSHU, THEN SHIKOKU.

THE TWO GREAT EARTHQUAKES TOOK DOWN THE TWO SOUTHERN ISLANDS, AND EVEN THE MAIN ISLAND HONSHU SUFFERED DAMAGE.

THOSE WHO SURVIVED CREATED SELF-GOVERNING STATES AMONG THE RUINS,

AND LIVE IN FEAR OF A THIRD EARTHQUAKE.

EXCEPT FOR A CERTAIN GROUP OF YOUNG MEN AND WOMEN.

PEEP PEEP

YES SIR.

WE'LL HEAD OVER IMMEDIATELY.

NATURAL DISASTERS AND GIANT CREATURES.
IT'S QUITE THE ADVENTURE.
AGAIN?
THEY'VE BEEN APPEARING A LOT LATELY.
THUMP
VROOM
BUT IT'S NOT SO BAD.
NO ONE TELLING US WHAT TO DO.
YEP.
AS LONG AS WE HAVE THIS POWER, WE'VE GOT NO WORRIES.
NO MATTER...
...WHAT MONSTER WE GO UP AGAINST.

It's an atanan!
WHOOSH
AH-
OOF
AGGH!
RUN FOR YOUR LIVES!

HEY YOU!
WHY AREN'T YOU RUNNING AWAY?
IT'S POINTLESS.
NO HUMAN CAN ESCAPE.
ROAR
HUH?
MURMUR
It's NOA!

NOA will save us!

EERRK

PHEW!

IT'S OKAY NOW.

NOW THAT NOA IS HERE...

...I GUESS WE DON'T HAVE TO RUN ANYMORE.

NOA?
YOU DON'T KNOW THEM?
THEY TOOK CONTROL OF THIS AREA AFTER THE BIG QUAKE.

THEY'RE JUST KIDS, BUT THEY UNITED AND ORGANIZED THEMSELVES.
Get into position.
AND THEY ENJOY PLAYING ARMY.
Yes sir.
IT'S IRONIC THAT WE NEED THEM TO SURVIVE.

LOOK OVER THERE.
SEE THAT TALL TOWER?

THAT'S NOA HEADQUARTERS.
BEFORE THE QUAKES, IT WAS SOME GOVERNMENT RESEARCH FACILITY.

THERE WAS A RUMOR THAT THEY GOT THEIR HANDS INTO SOME PARANORMAL STUFF.
I GUESS THERE WAS SOME TRUTH TO THOSE RUMORS.

LOOK AT THOSE SOLDIERS.
THEY FLY IN THE AIR AND USE UNNATURAL POWERS.
WE CALL THOSE ATANAN MONSTERS,
BUT THOSE SOLDIERS ARE HARDLY ANY DIFFERENT.

OUR GOVERNMENT WAS OBSESSED WITH SCIENCE.
WHO KNOWS WHAT THEY WERE PLANNING TO DO WITH NOA.
NATURAL DISASTERS AND MONSTER ATTACKS...
IT'S LIKE GOD HIMSELF HAS ABANDONED US.

YOU WERE ABANDONED BY THE KAMUI.

ATANAN ENGAGED IN EDEN AREA 8! IT'S ADVANCING TOWARDS THE CITY CENTER.
ALL LEVEL B SOLDIERS UNDER TENSHO COMMAND, REPORT TO BATTLE STATIONS! THIS IS NOT A DRILL, REPEAT...
THIS OPERATION WILL BE COMMANDED BY THE TENSHO HERSELF. REPEAT...
LADY SUMIRE.
MMM.
LADY SUMIRE.
ROLL
....
WHAT?

THE ORDER TO BATTLE STATIONS WAS ISSUED.
I DON'T WANNA GO.
BUT THEY JUST SAID YOU'RE COMMANDING, LADY SUMIRE.
DON'T GO.

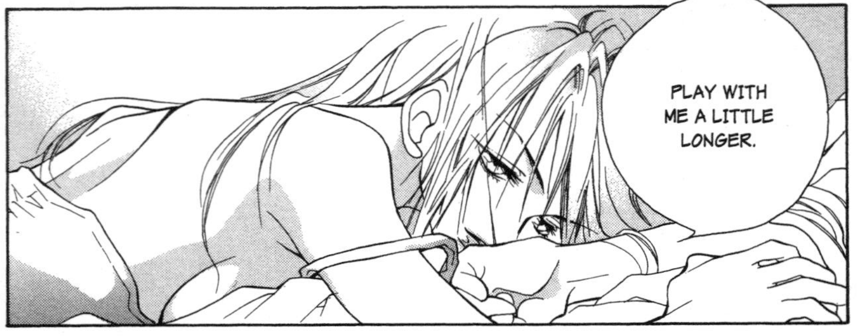
PLAY WITH ME A LITTLE LONGER.

ARE YOU SURE? WHAT ABOUT THE ORDER?
stroke
WHO CARES ABOUT THE ORDER?

I HAVE A STATION FOR YOU TO MAN HERE.

LADY SUMIRE.
SQUEAK
I HAVE A MESSAGE FROM GENERAL SHIKI.
YOU MUST PREPARE TO LEAVE AT ONCE.
Step
INCONSIDERATE AS USUAL,
AIKA.
EX-
EXCUSE ME MA'AM.
BYE-BYE.
DON'T DIE.

?

OH,
DON'T LOOK SO SERIOUS.
OR YOU'LL NEVER GET A MAN.
I CAN SET YOU UP...
...OR AREN'T YOU INTERESTED?
LADY SUMIRE...
YOUR CONDUCT...
...NOA RULES STATE THAT THERE ARE TO BE NO PERSONAL RELATIONSHIPS AMONG MEMBERS.
Hmph
IT'S OKAY.

I THOUGHT LIFE IN NOA WAS GOOD...
...BUT WITH A COMMANDER LIKE HER, LIFE IS GREAT!
HOW DID SHE BECOME A TOP COMMANDER, ANYWAY?
I HAVE PERMISSION.
APPROVED BY THE NOA GENERAL HIMSELF.
whistle ♪
THIS IS AWESOME!
tap
tap
Salute
SIR!
GENERAL SHIKI!

SLASH
SIR?
UNGH.
GEN...

...ERAL
tap
tap
SHIKI.
UNDERSTOOD.
PLEASE GET READY.
THIS ATANAN APPEARS TO BE STRONGER THAN BEFORE.
WITHOUT YOUR HELP, THEY...
WHAT'S THE POINT...
...OF FIGHTING THEM?

LADY SUMIRE?
WE SURVIVED THE EARTH-QUAKES.
BUT NOW WE LIVE IN FEAR OF GIANT BEASTS.

IT'S A LIFE WITH NO GUARANTEES.
SO WHAT'S THE POINT?
IF THAT'S ALL THERE IS...

...IT SHOULD ALL JUST END.

SCREEK

LADY SUMIRE?

OLD TOKYO AREA 1, ALSO KNOWN AS EDEN.
THE CITY SURVIVED THE EARTHQUAKES BECAUSE OF THE GOVERNMENT RESEARCH FACILITY'S BARRIER.
AND THOSE IGNORANT ADULTS WHO DIDN'T UNDERSTAND THE EXPERIMENTS...
...NOW BEG NOA TO SAVE THEIR LIVES.
THOSE FOOLS BELIEVE OUR POWER WILL SAVE THEM.
A ONCE FLOURISHING CAPITAL REDUCED TO A VILLAGE OF PITIFUL HUMANS.
DON'T YOU THINK THIS EXISTENCE IS WORTHLESS?

AS YOU SAY, WITHOUT NOA...
...NO ONE WOULD WANT TO SURVIVE.
BUT WE GAVE THOSE PEOPLE...

...THE DESIRE TO KEEP LIVING.

AND WITHIN THIS ORGANIZATION...
...YOU ARE ONE OF THE TOP THREE COMMANDERS, LADY SUMIRE.
Lift

I AM VERY HONORED TO SERVE UNDER YOUR DIRECT COMMAND.

YOU ARE EVERYTHING TO ME,

LADY SUMIRE.

OH, AIKA.

YOU'RE...

...SO SERIOUS.

I WILL BE OUTSIDE.
PLEASE CALL ME AS SOON AS YOU ARE READY TO LEAVE.
SURE.
I'M EVERYTHING?
CLICK
HAH!
I DON'T HAVE...
THAT MAKES ME LAUGH.
...ANYONE TO FEEL THAT WAY ABOUT.
EVERYONE LIVES FOR THEMSELVES.
Lift
I'M NO DIFFERENT.

SUMIRE.
GRAB
WHAT IS TAKING YOU SO LONG? HURRY.
....
YOU MUST FEEL IT TOO.
THIS...
I FEEL IT.
THE STRANGE WAVE THAT'S MOVING THROUGH THE CITY.

IF THIS WAVE BELONGS TO THE ATANAN, THEN IT'S MORE POWERFUL THAN ANY BEFORE.
YOU'RE SENDING ME OUT BECAUSE YOU WANT ME TO CHECK OUT THIS WAVE, RIGHT?
THERE'S NO WAY THE WEAKER SOLDIERS CAN DEFEAT IT.
Hmf
I TOLD HIM NOT TO DIE.
IF ANYONE FOUND OUT THAT THE LEADER OF NOA HIMSELF IS KILLING HIS OWN SOLDIERS,
IT COULD CAUSE A SCANDAL.
YOU AND I ARE THE SAME...
...GENERAL SHIKI.

THE ONE YOU REALLY WANT...
...IS THE ONE YOU'LL NEVER HAVE.
YOU MAY BE RIGHT.
THEN I KNOW WHAT I NEED TO DO.
I'M NOT HERE FOR THIS CITY.
KA-BOOM
I JUST WANT...
ROAR

ROAR
FLAP
WHAT'S GOING ON!?
THIS ONE IS DIFFERENT THAN OTHER ATANAN.
ARE THEY...
...HAVING TROUBLE FIGHTING IT?
BUT THEY'RE NOA.
MURMUR

ROAR
NO WAY!
WHAT'S GOING TO HAPPEN TO US!?

EXCUSE ME.
IT'S TIME TO STOP PLAYING AROUND.
STEP
OH.

CHEER
LADY SUMIRE!
IT'S LADY SUMIRE!
THAT WHITE UNIFORM MEANS SHE IS A TOP NOA COMMANDER.
IF SHE'S ONE OF THE TOP COMMANDERS, SHE'S POWERFUL, RIGHT?
MAYBE WE'LL STILL BE OKAY.

C'MON, CUTIE.
FLAP
I'LL PLAY WITH YOU.♡
ROAR

VOOSH
TAP
TAP
FLOAT

HEY, ATANAN.
IS THE WAVE THAT'S...
...MOVING THROUGH THIS CITY YOURS?
TELL ME.
WHOOSH

TOO BAD.
I GUESS IT WASN'T YOU.
GLOP GLOP
!
ビチャッ
Splat
HOW BORING.
THAT WAS NOTHING.
Shiver
YES, I CAN FEEL...
lick
...A POWER THAT MAKES MY HEART ACHE.

I DON'T LIKE CLEANING UP.
YES MA'AM!
I'LL LEAVE THE REST TO YOU BOYS.
step
Hmf
SILENCE
....
AFTER THEY BEG FOR HELP, THEIR EYES STILL FEAR THOSE WHO ARE DIFFERENT.
WEAKLINGS!

BUT THAT WAVE BOTHERS ME.
IF IT WASN'T FROM THE ATANAN, WHAT IS IT?
DID SHIKI AND I MAKE A MISTAKE?
NO, IT CAN'T BE.
BECAUSE I CAN SENSE IT A LITTLE EVEN NOW.
WHO IS THE OWNER OF THIS WAVE?
TWITCH
THE ATANAN...
...ISN'T DEAD!

LADY SUMIRE!
GASP

SLASH

I FOUND YOU.
THERE'S NO MISTAKING IT.
HUMANS USING THE FAKE TOHSU!
IT'S THE WAVE!

Chapter 02 *a traveler from the north*

WHIRRRRR

HE SLICED THROUGH THAT ATANAN WITH ONE BLOW?
GLOP
WHO IS THIS GUY?
SQUISH
FLICK
!?

POINT
LADY SUMIRE!

CHUNK
WHERE IS WHAT?
DID I...
...STEAL YOUR LOVER OR SOMETHING?
DON'T PLAY DUMB.
WOMAN WHO WIELDS THE POWER OF THE WIND I'TOUREN.
YOU CANNOT USE TOHSU AND NOT KNOW.

YOU...

GET BACK, LADY SUMIRE!
KOCHUK
HE KILLED THE ATANAN WITH ONE BLOW AND KNOWS THE WORD TOHSU.
HE IS NOT AN ORDINARY CITIZEN!

THERE'S NO NEED.
NO.
WE MUST PROTECT THE SECRETS OF NOA.

WE WILL FOLLOW NOA REGULATIONS AND...
CLICK
...ELIMINATE ANY THREAT!
RAT
TAT
TAT
TAT
TAT
TAT
TAT
TAT

IF YOU WANNA SURVIVE IN EDEN...
...YOU SHOULDN'T DO ANYTHING SUSPICIOUS IN FRONT OF US.

What!?

WHOOSH

NO WAY!

SCRUNCH

CZICK

DOES THIS GUY HAVE TOHSU TOO!?

WOOM

WHAT!?
VOOOSH
AS I SAID...
...THERE'S NO NEED TO INTERVENE.
WEEEEEE

CRASH

......

YOU NEEDN'T HAVE BOTHERED.

SAME GOES FOR YOU.

IF YOU WEREN'T PLANNING TO SAVE ME...

...THEN WHY DID YOU REVEAL YOURSELF...

WHY ARE YOU HERE...
...AND THAT POWER?

...AND WHERE DID YOU COME FROM?

I COME FROM THE FAR NORTH.
TO TAKE BACK THE "MIRACLE."

I SEE.

I'LL TAKE CARE OF HIM.
YOU BOYS HEAD BACK.
AND YOU DON'T NEED TO REPORT THIS TO SHIKI.
BUT LADY SUMIRE!

DID YOU HEAR ME?
YOU WILL OBEY MY ORDERS.
NEXT TIME...
...YOU WON'T GET A WARNING.
SHIVER

TH-
THEN...
...WE'LL
GET
GOING!
shink
THUMP
THUMP

I DON'T PLAN ON STAYING IN THIS MESSY PLACE.

LET'S GO WHERE WE CAN TALK PRIVATELY.

step

COMING, MR. TRAVELER FROM THE NORTH?

I DON'T PLAN ON DISCUSSING ANYTHING WITH YOU.
I JUST NEED TO KNOW WHERE IT'S HIDDEN.
THAT'S ALL YOU'VE SAID.
COULD YOU EXPLAIN IT TO ME FROM THE START?
OR ELSE HOW CAN I ANSWER YOU?
WE HAVE THE SAME POWERS.
IT'S NOT THE SAME.
IT IS THE SAME.

WE ARE HUMANS WITH THE POWER OF MONSTERS.
WHOOSH

YOU'RE A REPLICA.

A REPLICA? THAT'S INTERESTING.
WHY DO YOU SAY THAT?

YOU DON'T KNOW ANYTHING?
EVEN THOUGH YOU USE TOHSU?

LET ME TELL YOU ONE THING.
CAN YOU SEE THAT GIANT TOWER IN THE MIDDLE OF THE CITY?

THAT'S THE GOVERNMENT RESEARCH FACILITY THAT PROTECTED THIS AREA FROM THE EARTHQUAKES.
THAT ESTABLISHMENT HELD THE OLD GOVERNMENT'S HIGHEST TECHNOLOGY AND POWER.

AND THE WHITE SHELL ATTACHED TO IT IS NOA.
IT'S AN ORGANIZATION BACKED BY THE RESEARCH FACILITY TO PROTECT THE CITY FROM THE ATANAN.
IT'S THE ORGANIZATION I BELONG TO.

A CHAINED DOG, HUH?
NO, A GUINEA PIG.

WE ARE GUINEA PIGS IMPLANTED WITH THESE POWERS...
...BY THE RESEARCH FACILITY.

TO NOA, THE RESEARCH FACILITY IS...
...THE SOURCE OF OUR POWER.
THAT'S WHY WE DON'T KNOW ANYTHING.

WE ATTAINED THIS POWER...
...BY SELLING OUR OWN BODIES.
WHOOSH
WE ENDURE SECRET EXPERIMENTS.
REPEATS OF PAIN AND PLEASURE. AND ONLY THOSE WHO SHOW RESULTS ARE SELECTED.
THAT'S NOA.
WE FIGHT AS ORDERED.
AND THE ONLY WAY TO KEEP OUR POWER IS...
...TO CONTINUE BEING THEIR GUINEA PIGS.

WHY DON'T YOU TRY TO BREAK THOSE CHAINS?

ONCE YOU GAIN THE POWER...

...YOUR SENSE OF JUSTICE IS PARALYZED.

NO MATTER WHAT YOU DO, IT'S BETTER THAN BEING A WEAK HUMAN.

THE WORLD IS FALLING APART. BUT AS LONG AS YOU HAVE POWER, YOU CAN DO SOMETHING.

IF YOU GIVE UP YOUR BODY TO GAIN ALL THAT... I GUESS THAT'S ENOUGH.

MAYBE THAT'S OUR JUSTIFICATION.
....

LADY SUMIRE.
STEP

PLEASE STOP.
BOW

I CANNOT LET YOU DISCLOSE THE SECRETS OF NOA...
...EVEN IF YOU ARE A TOP COMMANDER.

AND YOU.
STEP
I WON'T ALLOW YOU NEAR LADY SUMIRE FROM NOW ON.

PLEASE.
LET'S GO BACK, LADY SUMIRE.

FLINCH

COME JOIN NOA.

WHAT!?

WHAT ARE YOU SAYING!?

YOU SAID YOU'RE SEARCHING FOR A MIRACLE.
DON'T YOU THINK...
...NOA'S POWERS ARE RATHER MIRACULOUS?

I DON'T KNOW WHAT YOU'RE LOOKING FOR.

BUT...

...YOU MUST FEEL A CONNECTION TO US...

...FOR YOU TO HAVE COME HERE NOW.

IF YOU WANT TO MOVE AROUND FREELY, YOU SHOULD JOIN THE BIG KIDS.

IN THIS CITY, NOA IS THE TOP.

YOU CAN FIND LOTS OF INFORMATION.

LIKE...

...GOVERNMENT SECRETS.

—

YOU WANT ME TO BE YOUR LAPDOG?

THAT ISN'T IT.
TOUCH
I MEAN...
...I WANT TO HELP YOU.

SHUDDER
LADY SUMIRE!
BOOM!

SHY, IS HE?

I GUESS HE DOESN'T LIKE ME.

LADY SUMIRE, ARE YOU HURT!?

DASH

DON'T WORRY.

JUST A SCRATCH.

HE HAS A POWER THAT RIVALS THE BEST OF NOA.

WHO IS HE?

LET'S HEAD BACK, AIKA.
ONCE I REACH FOR IT ...

....
YES MA'AM.

...I WON'T LET IT GO.

tap
tap
tap

DID YOU HAVE TROUBLE? IT TOOK YOU LONG ENOUGH.

DID YOU FIND THE OWNER OF THE WAVE?

THE ATANAN ARE GROWING STRONGER EVERY TIME.
BUT WE COULDN'T FIGURE OUT WHAT THAT WAVE WAS.
SUMIRE.

WHAT HAPPENED?
TUG
HEY,
SHIKI.
WHAT DO YOU GAIN BY BEING CHAINED...
...TO NOA?
WHAT A QUESTION...
...SUMIRE.
YOU DON'T KNOW THE ANSWER?

tap

THERE'S NOTHING THAT NEEDS...

...TO BE REPORTED TO YOU, SHIKI.

tap

tap

SE-SBOW 3rd
PLEASE EXCUSE ME, GENERAL SHIKI.
BOW
AIKA.

YOU MUST ELIMINATE ANY DANGER TO SUMIRE.

THAT'S THE RESPONSIBILITY OF THE TENSHO LIEUTENANT.
YES SIR!
tap
tap

WHAT ARE YOU PLANNING, LADY SUMIRE?

GENERAL SHIKI IS ALREADY SUSPICIOUS.

WHAT DO YOU PLAN ON DOING WITH THAT PERSON?

AIKA.

PULL UP THE CEP DATA ON THE MONITOR.

THE CEP?
WHAT EVER FOR?
I JUST WANT TO CHECK SOMETHING.

creak
click
clack
click

file/code:001397658-a207
file name/the conservation of
environment project
level/sss safty device operatic
now checking...
file/code:001397658-a207
file name/the conservation of
environment project
level/sss safty device operation
HRMMMM

READ IT TO ME.

?

Plip
WHIRRR

code/001397658a-207
!CAUTION
closed area
intrusion
out line of
this proj
THE GOVERNMENT SET UP A RE-LOCATION PROGRAM TEN YEARS AGO.
IN ORDER TO SLOW DOWN THE REDUCTION OF NATURAL HABITAT DUE TO URBAN SPRAWL,
A NATIONAL CONSERVATION PROGRAM, CALLED CEP.
THE LOCATION WAS OLD HOKKAIDO. THE PROJECT WAS COMPLETED AS PLANNED FIVE YEARS AGO. THIS WAS BEFORE THE FIRST SINKER.
THE CONSERVATION OF THE ENVIRONMENT PROJECT
IT WAS CLOSED OFF AS THE ONLY NATIONAL PARK WITH NATURAL HABITAT IN THE COUNTRY.
NOT EVEN GOVERNMENT OFFICIALS ARE ALLOWED TO ENTER.
WHAT'S THE CURRENT STATUS?
IS IT POSSIBLE THAT PEOPLE LIVE THERE?
ACCORDING TO THE DATA, THERE ARE NONE.

BUT HE SAID...
...HE CAME FROM THE NORTH.

DO YOU USUALLY BELIEVE EVERYTHING A STRANGER TELLS YOU?

I LIKE MYSTERIOUS MEN.
hee hee

THEN...
...YOU WERE SERIOUS WHEN YOU INVITED HIM TO JOIN NOA?

AIKA, DON'T YOU WANT TO KNOW?

WE HAVE THE POWER TO KILL MONSTERS.
BUT WE DON'T KNOW ANYTHING ABOUT THE EXPERIMENT.
NOTHING ABOUT WHAT WAS DONE TO OUR BODIES. WHAT MODIFICATIONS WERE MADE.

AND...
...WHAT THE SOURCE OF THE POWER IS.
HE IS...

...A CHANCE TO FIND THOSE ANSWERS.

AT THE LEAST,

OUR POWERS ARE SIMILAR.

FU

AND YOU BELIEVE THIS BECAUSE?

HE CALLED ME A REPLICA.

HOW COULD HE SAY THAT...

...UNLESS HE KNOWS THE ORIGINAL.

THE THING THAT IS IN OUR BODIES,
AND THE THING HE IS LOOKING FOR...
...MUST BE RELATED.

IF WE ARE...
...REPLICAS THRUST INTO THE REALM OF GODS...
...THEN HE MUST BE AN ORIGINAL FROM THAT REALM.
I DON'T WANT TO KNOW THE SOURCE OF THE POWER IF IT RISKS MY POSITION.
I HAVE THE SAME POWERS AS YOU, AND I CAN STAY BY YOUR SIDE.
AS LONG AS I HAVE THAT, THERE IS NOTHING ELSE I WISH FOR.

PLUS...
...I'M SCARED OF FINDING OUT.

BUT WHAT I DON'T UNDERSTAND IS...

...YOU GAVE UP YOUR OWN BODY TO THE EXPERIMENT AND JOINED NOA.

AND YOU ATTAINED ONE OF THE HIGHEST POSITIONS HERE.

EVERYONE IN NOA ENVIES YOUR STRONG POWERS.

YOU ARE THE ULTIMATE ACHIEVEMENT.

I DON'T UNDERSTAND WHY YOU ARE SO INTERESTED IN THAT PERSON...

...THAT YOU WOULD RISK ALL YOU HAVE ATTAINED.

IT'S BECAUSE...

SQUEAK

HE'S THE ONLY ONE WHO HAS EVER USED THE WORD...

..."MIRACLE."
HIS PIERCING EYES.
THERE'S SOMETHING ALIKE ABOUT US.
THE WORLD HAS GONE INSANE ALREADY ANYWAY.
THE WORDS ON HIS LIPS.
AND THAT'S WHY I'M INTERESTED IN HIM.
EVEN NOW, THERE'S A PART OF ME...
...THAT STILL LONGS FOR A MIRACLE.

ATSUMA.

THAT WOMAN'S OFFER...

...ISN'T A BAD IDEA.

WHY ARE YOU HESITATING?

YOU HAVEN'T FORGOTTEN OUR MISSION, HAVE YOU?

OR...

...ARE YOU SCARED OF THAT WOMAN?

SHUT UP.
HEHEH. OH YEAH.
YOU ASKED HER SOMETHING INTERESTING.
GRIP
"WHY DON'T YOU TRY TO BREAK THOSE CHAINS?" YOU ASKED.
WHAT ABOUT YOU, ATSUMA?
DON'T YOU WANT TO ESCAPE FROM ME?
He heh
GRIP
SCRATCH
I SAID SHUT UP!

SHOW IT TO ME.

N-001
ORGANIZA-TION...
...BOUND IN CHAINS.

IF THERE REALLY IS A MIRACLE.

Chapter
03 fortress of monsters

THE GREAT EARTH IS WEEPING WITH ANGER...

...AND SORROW, SINCE IT'S SPIRIT WAS TAKEN AWAY.

Neither kamui nor human, it is a living "miracle," child of love.

ATSUMA.
YOU MUST BRING THE GREAT EARTH'S SPIRIT BACK...
...BEFORE TIME RUNS OUT.
THIS TASK IS YOUR DESTINY.

No one may touch it.

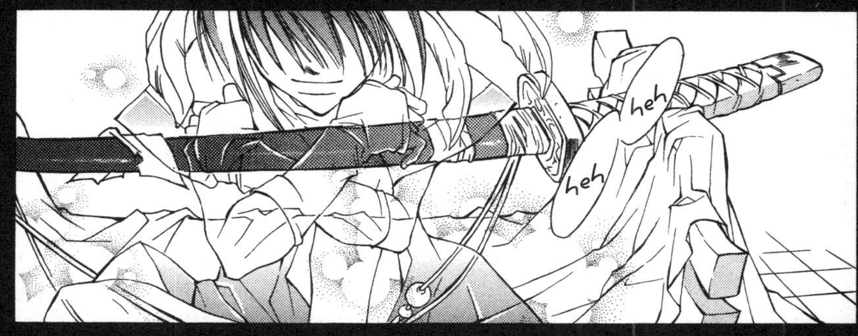

Doom to those who break the covenant.

heh
heh

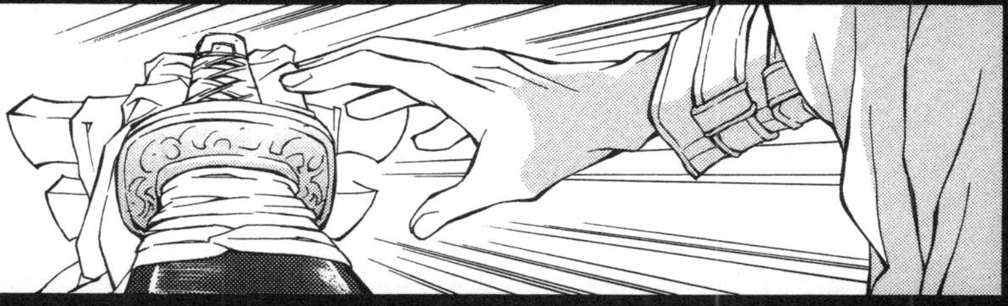

The great earth will shake, and withdraw it's protective hand.

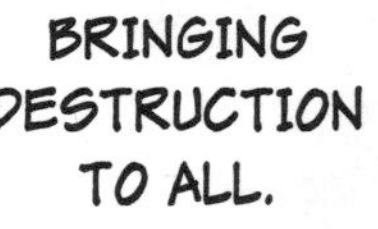
BRINGING DESTRUCTION TO ALL.

chirp
chirp

SCRUNCH
ARE YOU GOING?

SQUEAK
FOR THE VERY IMPORTANT TASK? IN ORDER TO STOP THE DESTRUCTION?

C'MON, TELL ME.
EVER OBEDIENT ATSUMA.
SPLASH

STEP
WHY DO YOU CARE?

HMM...
DID YOU KNOW?
YOU'RE THE ONLY ONE...
...I ALLOW TO DO THIS...
Paint
...SHUI.

I KNOW.

YOU'RE NOT GOING TO SAY...
whump
..."I'M HONORED?"

I KNOW THAT YOU DON'T NEED SILLY WORDS LIKE THAT.
SQUEEZE
ALL YOU NEED IS THIS.

Hmf
WHAT MAKES YOU THINK THAT?
DON'T YOU REMEMBER?
MY TOHSU HAS TELEPATHIC ABILITIES.

BUT I CAN'T SEE WHAT HAPPENED TO THIS HAND.

Smile

IT WAS A STRAY CAT.

THEN NEXT TIME YOU SEE THAT CAT,

I'LL TAME IT FOR YOU. I'M AN ANIMAL LOVER.

IT LOOKS LIKE YOUR HIGHNESS REALLY LIKED THAT CAT.

Hee hee

IS THAT YOUR TELEPATHY TOO?

WHO ARE YOU, REALLY?
AN ANIMAL LOVING TELEPATH?
MAYBE YOU SHOULDN'T ASK SO MUCH. IF YOU GET TOO INTERESTED, I MIGHT GET KILLED.

Whisper
BY THE KING.

LADY SUMIRE.
IT IS TIME TO GO.
step

I'M A WORRYWART.
Grin

DON'T GLARE AT ME LIKE THAT.
DON'T WORRY.

I WON'T LAY A FINGER ON YOU.

YOU'RE EXCUSED!
YES MA'AM.

BUT BEFORE I GO,
MAY I ASK LADY SUMIRE A QUESTION?
drip
WAS THE CAT WHO SCRATCHED YOU,
WEARING BLACK AND CARRYING A SWORD?

MORE LIKE AN ABANDONED CAT...
...THAN A STRAY.
grin

SHOULD I BRING YOU SOME MILK AND A TOWEL?
AREN'T YOU GOING TO SCRATCH ME?
tap
tap

I GUESS HE MEANT IT.
WHEN HE SAID HE LIKES ANIMALS.
ANYWAY.
I HAVE A NEW TASK FOR YOU, AIKA.
CAN YOU SHOW OUR NEW RECRUIT AROUND?
GET HIM A UNIFORM AND A ROOM TOO.
!

THAT'S AN ORDER, UNDERSTAND?

....
YES MA'AM.
WELCOME TO NOA.

MAY I ASK YOU YOUR NAME?
I'M SUMIRE.

......
I'M ATSUMA.

HMM, ATSUMA.
YOU ARE GOING TO BE A THREAT TO NOA, AREN'T YOU?
BUT LET'S NOT TALK ABOUT THAT.

I'M NOT NICE ENOUGH TO GIVE YOU A HELPING HAND...

...WITHOUT ASKING SOMETHING IN RETURN.

Hee hee
IT'S NOT SUCH A BAD DEAL.
Skwick
I ONLY WANT ONE THING.
THUMP

I BROUGHT YOU TO NOA.
SO I WANT YOU TO SHOW ME.

I DON'T CARE WHAT FORM IT'S IN.
THE "MIRACLE" YOU TALK ABOUT.

NOBLE OFFENSIVE ACADEMY.

NOA FOR SHORT.

AN ORGANIZATION CREATED TO FIGHT THE ATANAN. THIS IS ALSO THE CITY CENTER.

BOW
no.1-6
control of
the executives
no admittance area

BRIDGE

SPECIAL RO
auditorium/

THE SIX BRIDGES ARE THE STUDENT LIVING QUARTERS.

THERE'S A LOUNGE BETWEEN THE MAIN OPERATION AREAS IN THE MIDDLE THAT INCLUDES SPECIALIZED FACILITIES.

OUR MAIN TASK IS TO PROTECT THE CITY.

WE ARE ALLOWED TO HANDLE ARMED VEHICLES FOR THAT PURPOSE.

THE STUDENTS ARE RANKED BY THEIR POTENTIAL POWER AND EXPERIENCE POINTS.

YOUR TREATMENT DEPENDS ON YOUR RANK.

THERE ARE THREE TOP COMMANDERS.
UNDER THEM ARE ASSISTANT OFFICERS CALLED TEN-I AND CHI-I.
AT THE BOTTOM ARE CADETS.
OVER HERE IS THE BATTLE TRAINING TOWER.
TOHSU PRACTICE IS HERE.
TOHSU, HUH?
SHE DIDN'T SEEM TO KNOW THE ESSENCE OF TOHSU AT ALL.
WHEN THE RESEARCH FACILITY RECRUITED PEOPLE FOR NOA,
THERE WERE ONLY TWO REQUIREMENTS. A YOUNG, HEALTHY BODY THAT COULD WITHSTAND THE EXPERIMENT, AND YOUR OWN DESIRE.
BUT THE NATURE OF THE EXPERIMENT WAS NEVER EXPLAINED TO US. NOT EVEN THE TOP COMMANDERS.

GATE/04
BUT AT THE END, WE HAD THESE POWERS.
THE RESEARCHERS CALLED IT TOHSU.

BANG
SO THEY WERE KIND ENOUGH TO GIVE YOU A NAME.

JUST TO KEEP YOU FROM ASKING MORE QUESTIONS.
YOU WON'T BE ABLE TO FIGHT THE ATANAN FOREVER.
WHETHER IT'S FOR JUSTICE OR POWER, IT'S STILL A WASTE.

Hmph!
DON'T TALK AS IF YOU KNOW.
WHY WOULD SOMEONE SACRIFICE SO MUCH FOR THIS SORT OF LIFE?
THE PAY. CURIOSITY. POWER. THERE ARE PLENTY OF REASONS.
WHAT ARE YOUR REASONS?

I DON'T WANT ANYTHING.
THE EXPERIMENT AND THE ATANAN,
ARE JUST REASONS TO STAY BY LADY SUMIRE'S SIDE.
peep

IT'S TIME.
WE'LL GO TO THE GENERAL ASSEMBLY HALL.
....

THE TOP COMMANDERS ARE THREE PEOPLE WHO SHOWED EXCEPTIONAL ABILITIES IN THE INITIAL RESEARCH PHASE.
TO RULE NOA...
tap
tap
...IS TO RULE THIS CITY.

CREAK

MANY HAVE TRIED TO WREST CONTROL FROM THEM.
BUT EVERYONE CAME TO FEAR THEIR AWESOME POWER.
THEY ARE...
glitter
...THE PINNACLE OF EXISTENCE.
NOA
Noble Offe.
Acad
VWOON

sizzle
ROAR
SILENCE
LIFT
THE OLD ERA...
...SANK WITH THE EARTHQUAKE.

THOSE WHO ARE HERE NOW...

...HAVE A NEW POWER.

NOA

WAVE

THE DISASTER THAT SANK KYUUSHU AND SHIKOKU AND HALTED THE OPERATIONS OF THIS COUNTRY,

THE GRAND SINKER.

IF YOU WISH TO THINK OF IT AS GOD'S JUDGMENT, SO BE IT.

WITH THE THREAT OF A THIRD SINKER AND APPEARANCE OF THE ATANAN,

THIS WORLD IS ON THE BRINK OF DESTRUCTION.

THE ADULTS WHO PREACHED FREEDOM WHILE OPPRESSING US COULD NOT ADAPT...
...AND BECAME WEAKLINGS WHO BEG US FOR HELP.
NOW THERE IS NO ONE TO CHALLENGE NOA, AND THIS WORLD HAS BECOME OUR CUSTOM-MADE PARADISE.

SO WHY SHOULD WE BE OBLIGATED TO ANYONE?

ENJOY THIS BRIEF MOMENT OF FREEDOM. DESTROY THE THREAT OF THE ATANAN.
TAKE WHAT YOU WANT, KILL WHO YOU WANT, AND BE STRONG!
IN THESE UNCERTAIN TIMES, NO ONE CAN SAVE YOU BUT YOURSELF.

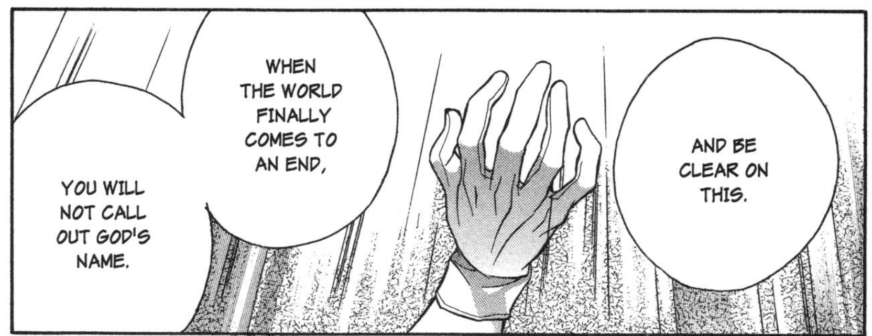
AND BE CLEAR ON THIS.
WHEN THE WORLD FINALLY COMES TO AN END,
YOU WILL NOT CALL OUT GOD'S NAME.

You will call out your own name!
NOA
Noble Offensive Academy
ROAR
CHEER

SHE'S...
...A TOP COMMANDER?

THE THREE PEOPLE ON THE STAGE ARE...

...GENERAL SHIKI.

THE CHISHO, LORD HYDE. AND THE TENSHO, LADY SUMIRE.

NOA IS RUN ON THEIR AUTHORITY AND BALANCE OF POWER.

A SONG?

WHERE IS IT COMING FROM?

GASP

THIS VOICE!

IT SOUNDS JUST LIKE...

IT CAN'T BE!

IS IT ...!?
peek
OH?
tsk
tsk
THE KITTY CAT CAME TO HEAR MY SONG.

……
SHOULD I SING SOMETHING FOR YOU?
KITTY CAT?

WERE YOU DRAWN TO MY VOICE?
YOU'VE GOT TO BE KIDDING.
YOU'RE NOT NICE.

YOU HEARD HIS WORSHIPFUL-NESS' ROYAL SPEECH, HUH?
IT'S NOT MY CUP OF TEA.
BUT THERE ARE PLENTY WHO WANT TO GET NEAR THE TOP COMMANDERS.

IF YOU WERE RECRUITED BY LADY SUMIRE DIRECTLY, YOU HAVE HER INTEREST.
YOU CAN USE THAT TO YOUR ADVANTAGE.
I'M NOT LIKE YOU.

I DON'T KNOW WHAT YOU HOPE TO GAIN BY FAWNING OVER HER,
I DON'T PLAN ON BECOMING A LAPDOG.
ME?
SHE'S ONLY THINKING ABOUT HER OWN DESIRES.
BUT I WOULDN'T BE CAUGHT DEAD WITH THAT WOMAN.
...CAUGHT YOU.
I...
ReaCH

!
YOU DON'T...
...KNOW ANYTHING.

YOU DON'T KNOW...
URGH.
...ANYTHING ABOUT HER.
grab
CHOKE
THUD
GAH.

I'M SHUI.

AIKA HAS PUT ME IN CHARGE OF YOU.

NICE TO MEET YOU.

ATSUMA.

HIS VOICE.

YOU'RE SCRAWNY, AREN'T YOU?

ARE YOU REALLY AN ABANDONED CAT?

rub rub

I GUESS I'LL JUST HAVE TO FATTEN YOU UP WITH MY AMAZING COOKING SKILLS.

IT'LL BE LIKE HAVING A LITTLE BRO...

tap

TURN
くるん
THUMP
LANDED ON YOUR FEET.
He's a kitty cat alright.
MY GOODNESS...
...LADY SUMIRE.
I REALLY WANT TO TAME HIM NOW.

ZZZZAA

squeak

SO...

...WHAT DO YOU THINK?

DO THE KIDS GETTING HIGH FROM ALL THIS POWER...

...GIVE YOU THE CREEPS?

NO.

swish

I DON'T...
...GET THE CREEPS.

THAT'S GOOD.
IF YOU ACCEPT MY OFFER...
...WILL YOU SHOW ME SOMETHING IN RETURN TOO?

OKIKURUMI.

WHAT'S THAT?

AN ANCIENT LIVING BEING.

IT'S BEEN SAID THAT IT HAS THE POWER OF A MIRACLE.

IT'S SUPPOSED TO BE HERE.

MY OBJECTIVE...

...IS TO TAKE BACK OKIKURUMI.

IS THAT...
...RELATED TO THE RESEARCH EXPERIMENT?
shiver

ARE YOU SURE...
...YOU WANT TO TELL ME ALL THIS?

I DON'T THINK YOU COMMANDERS TALK.

HEE HEE. YOU WERE ABLE TO FIGURE THAT OUT?
YES. SHIKI DOESN'T CARE WHAT I DO.

I WAS JUST THINKING HOW I WANT TO SHATTER THAT ROYAL ATTITUDE OF HIS.
BY THE WAY, ATSUMA.

Step
CAN YOU...

...FIGURE ME OUT, TOO?

!!

I HAVE...

MAKE NO MISTAKE.

DON'T TOUCH ME!

SLAP

...NO INTENTION OF COOPERATING WITH YOU PEOPLE.
CRACKLE
step
LADY SUMIRE!
WE DON'T KNOW HIS REAL INTENTION!
HE'S TOO DANGER-OUS!
WELL, I GUESS...
I KNEW THAT FROM THE BEGIN-NING.
WHAT!?
Hmf
I GUESS HE NEEDS DINNER AND A MOVIE FIRST.

ARE YOU SPYING ON THE TENSHO AGAIN?
pshhht
GENERAL.
YOU'RE SO SERIOUS.
tap
tap
THERE'S NOT MUCH DATA ON HIM.
IS HE A SPY FROM THE RESEARCH LAB?
I CAN'T SAY FOR SURE ONE WAY OR ANOTHER.
L LIST
Atsuma(surname unknown)
16(birthdate unknown)
SEX Male
BLOOD TYPE unknown
ABILITY no data
CAPACITY same as stated adove
EXPERIENCE same as stated adove
NOTES scarcely data require obtaining one
WELL, WE CAN'T COMPLAIN SINCE WE CAN DO ANYTHING WE WANT.
BUT WE SHOULD MAKE HIM FEEL AT HOME.
SO WHEN SHOULD WE KILL HIM?

NO,

I'M CONCERNED ABOUT SUMIRE'S INTENTIONS TOO.

I'M GOING TO LET HIM MOVE ABOUT FREELY.

ISN'T THAT KIND OF YOU.

sizzle

Heh.

WELL, WELL.

SWEET GENERAL.

THEN YOU'RE GOING TO LET ME PLAY ON MY OWN TOO, RIGHT?

tap

tap

I DON'T LIKE THAT CHICK,

BUT SHE HAS GOOD TASTE.

SOMETIMES MEAT'S BETTER WHEN IT'S A MYSTERY.

step

I WONDER...

...HOW HE TASTES?

DIRTY BASTARD.

I WONDER WHICH ORGANIZATION...
...IS BACKING UP THAT GUY?
IT DOESN'T MATTER.
HE'S GOING TO SHAKE THINGS UP AROUND HERE.
DON'T YOU THINK...
...THAT'S GOOD ENOUGH?
PLUS,
WE LEARNED SOMETHING ABOUT THE RESEARCH FACILITY'S SECRETS.

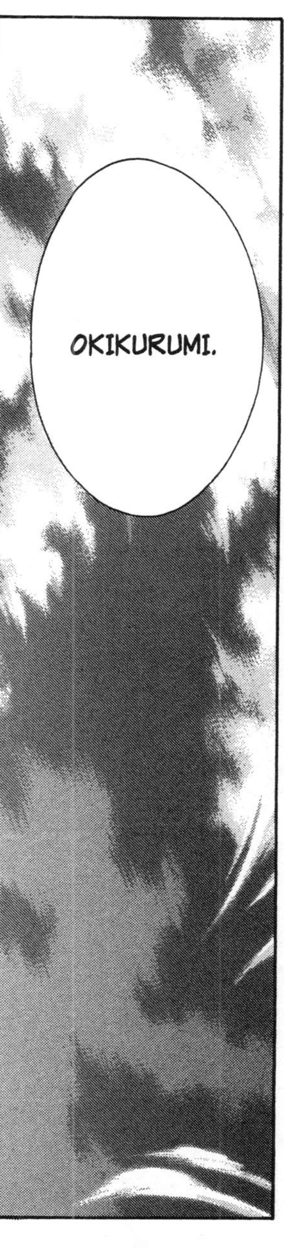
OKIKURUMI.

WHY DID YOU TELL THAT LADY SO MUCH?
YOU AREN'T REALLY SURE, ARE YOU?

DO YOU LIKE THAT LADY, ATSUMA?
OR IS IT THAT OTHER GUY?

Heheh
STILL CHASING HIS SHADOW?
NO!

I DON'T HAVE PROOF YET...
...BUT I CAN FEEL IT.

THE ONE WHO CREATES MIRACLES, OKIKURUMI...
...IS HERE.

Chapter
04 the spy
KEEP OUT
TRESPAS
制限区
CONT
CAUTIO
CONTAINER
PLACED ON
LEVEL SUR
LOAD UNIF
LEVEL SURFACE
LOAD UNIFORMLY
→CONTROL ROOM
↑AUDITORIUM

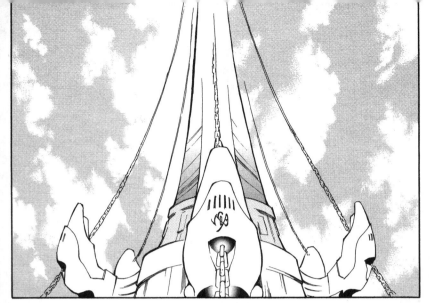

ATSUMA!
pshhht
IT'S TIME FOR YOUR MORNING MILK.

HMMM?
OUT FOR A WALK ALREADY?

I DON'T MIND THAT HE'S INDEPENDENT...
...BUT HE SHOULDN'T WALK AROUND BY HIMSELF WHEN HE JUST JOINED UP.

I GUESS I SHOULD HUNT DOWN...
...THE LOST KITTY.
A FEW DAYS AGO,
HE QUICKLY DEFEATED A FLYING ATANAN THAT APPEARED ON THE OUTSKIRTS OF THE CITY.
THE TENSHO, LADY SUMIRE LIKED HIS ABILITY. SHE RECRUITED HIM AND HE OFFICIALLY ENROLLED IN NOA.
HIS CURRENT CLASS IS TEN-I.
AND HIS PERSONAL DATA IS UNKNOWN.
IS HE YOUR NEXT PREY?
NAME
Atsuma(surname unknown)
16(birthdate unknown)
Male
unknown
no data
same as stated adove
same as stated adove
scarcely data
require obtaining one
0424/ny1975-25
S-ti/00773405
TEN-I
PERSONAL

LORD HYDE?

HE SEEMS TO POSSESS A POWER SIMILAR TO TOHSU.
YOU'RE AWFULLY INTERESTED IN HIM.
tug
YANAGI.

ARE YOU GOING TO REPLACE ME?

PUFF

rustle
I LIKE YOUR FINE HAIR.
BUT I LIKE TO TASTE SOMETHING ROUGHER FROM TIME TO TIME.

IF YOU BECOME ADDICTED, I MIGHT HAVE TO KILL YOU.
AS YOU LIKE.

I'M SICK OF DEVOURING THOSE IN NOA.
I WAS THINKING OF TASTING ATANAN,
BUT NOW THIS ONE SHOWS UP.
I WONDER...

...IF THAT CHICK WAS THINKING OF ME.
PUFF
THEN WHY DON'T YOU...
...THANK LADY SUMIRE, LORD HYDE...

...WITH A CORPSE...

...YOU SUCKED THE LIFE FROM?

AN EXCELLENT IDEA.
YOU HAVE GREAT TASTE AS USUAL...
...YANAGI.

PSSSSHT
SMIRK
NO MORE THAN YOU.

NICE LOOK.
step
ARE YOU GONNA LET ME SEE IT?

SW-S BOW 5th
THE THIRD FOOR

I HEAR YOU HAVE A PET YOU CAN'T TAME,

PRINCESS.

DO YOU WANT ME TO TRAIN IT?

Smile

YOU COULD GET YOUR THROAT TORN OUT.

THAT COULD BE COSTLY.

THIS ONE BITES.

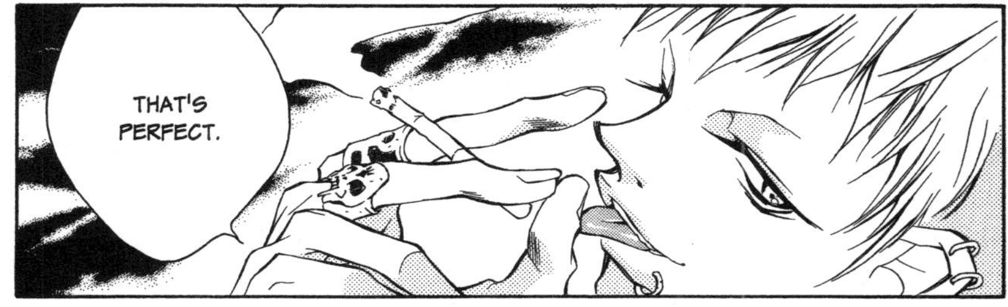

TURN
IT'D BE NO FUN IF HE DIDN'T LAST.
HE NEEDS TO SUFFER FIRST.
HOW ELSE CAN I GET OFF?
MY DOOR'S ALWAYS OPEN.
toss

FEEL FREE TO GIVE ME A CALL, PRINCESS.
tap
tap

STOMP
sizzle
THAT MAN...
...LACKS THE HONOR AND DIGNITY OF A TOP COMMANDER!
OH...
...IT DOESN'T MATTER.

I'M NOT WORRIED ABOUT LOSING MY NEW TOY...

...TO SOMEONE LIKE HIM.

THOUGH... I HAVEN'T SEEN HIM AT ALL THIS MORNING.

YOU HAVE NOTHING TO WORRY ABOUT.

I ASSIGNED SHUI TO TAKE CARE OF HIM.

AIKA.

YOU JUST DON'T UNDERSTAND.

?

I'M FAR MORE SUSPICIOUS...

...OF SOMEONE LIKE SHUI.

KEEP OUT

ENTER AND LOCK AGAIN IMEDIATERY

ERROR

click

clack

click

BEEP

BEEP

AN ERROR AGAIN?

JUST AS WE THOUGHT, SECURITY IS PRETTY TIGHT.
WE CAN'T CONNECT TO THE RESEARCH FACILITY FROM NOA.
HEH HEH. IT'S FUNNY, HUH?
MISSION

HUMANS ARE DESPERATELY USING TECHNOLOGY ...
...TO HIDE SOMETHING THAT CANNOT WORK WITH SCIENCE.

BUT IT'S BEING REJECTED.
MAYBE THIS IS PAYBACK...
...FOR CUTTING THEMSELVES OFF FROM THE WORLD.

KNOW WHAT?
カチッ
CLICK

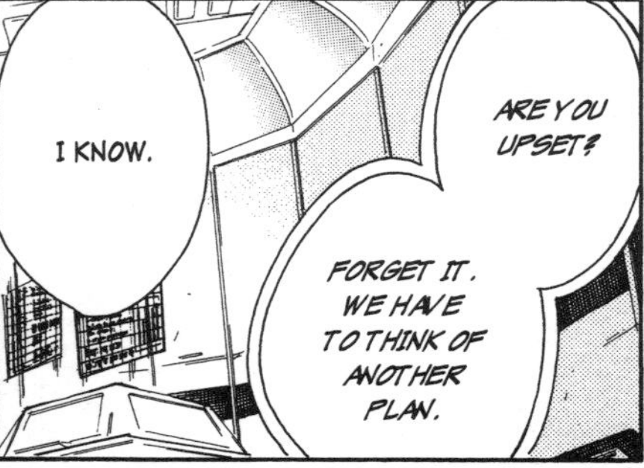
ARE YOU UPSET?
I KNOW.
FORGET IT. WE HAVE TO THINK OF ANOTHER PLAN.

I WANTED TO MEET THE NEW RECRUIT WHO'S DRAWING THE ATTENTION OF THE TOP COMMANDERS.

NICE TO MEET YOU, ATSUMA.

BUT...

...YOU SHOULDN'T BE NAUGHTY.
THESE FELLOWS VOLUNTEERED TO HAVE THEIR BODIES MODIFIED.
GRRRRR
WE CALL THEM MAGATSU-HEI.
ARRRGG
THE MODIFICATIONS WENT TOO FAR AND THEIR BRAINS ARE MUSH NOW...
KACHUNK
...BUT PLAY NICE ANYWAY.

GROWL

!

THERE'S NO POINT IN KILLING HUMANS WHO DON'T UNDERSTAND TOHSU,

AND LET THEMSELVES BE ENSLAVED.

CLANG

MAYBE FOR YOU.

WOBBLE
WHAT A HASSLE.
WHAT DO YOU WANT TO DO...
...ATSUMA?
DAMN.
ARGH!
BOOM
!?

THUD
THUD
...WHERE
IS...

...YOUR
HOME?

ZLISH
Woof.
The watch dog has arrived.

WELL, WELL.
THE INFAMOUS TEN-I OFFICER SHUI.
DID YOU WANT SOMETHING?
step
swish
I CAME TO LOOK FOR MY LOST CAT.
OH, I DIDN'T KNOW YOU WERE THE HANDLER.
tap
tap
IF HE'S SUCH A PRECIOUS CAT, MAYBE YOU SHOULD PUT A LEASH ON HIM.
ARE THESE THINGS YOUR IDEA OF A CAT TOY?
THUMP
KICK
ESPECIALLY IF IT'S A RARE BREED.

THIS LOOKS LIKE AN AMBUSH TO ME.

IT'S AN AWFUL LOT TO GO THROUGH FOR JUST ONE CAT.

I DON'T THINK EVEN YOU'D BE ABLE TO GET AWAY WITH IT...

...CHISHO LIEUTENANT AND RESIDENT GENIUS.
YANAGI.

PUSH
YOU OF ALL PEOPLE...
...FORGOT THE NUMBER ONE RULE?

THOSE WITH POWER MAKE THE RULES.
THAT'S THE MEANING OF EXISTENCE AT NOA.

BAM

OH GEEZ.

WHAT A BAD KITTY.

THUD

THUD

THAT WOMAN GAVE ME

THE FREEDOM TO MOVE AROUND THE FACILITY.

WHAT ARE YOU THINKING,
GETTING YOURSELF INVOLVED IN THIS?
ARE YOU...

...WORRIED ABOUT ME?
KICK

HEY.

YOU KNOW THAT THESE GUYS HAVE NO INDEPENDENT THOUGHT RIGHT?
I DON'T THINK THEY'D BE UPSET IF YOU KILLED THEM.
FLARE

UNLESS YOU HAVE ANOTHER IDEA.
THUMP

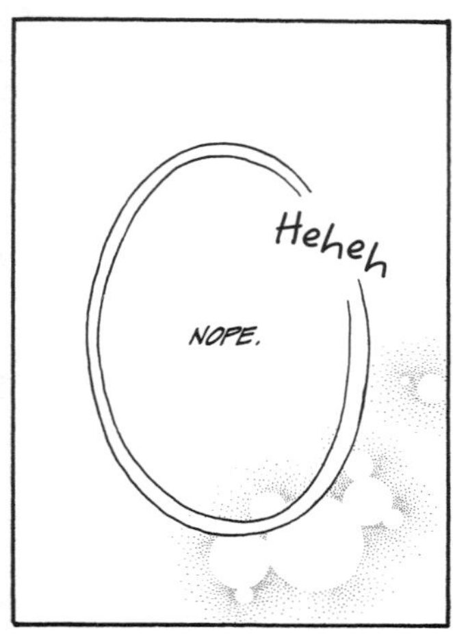
Heheh
NOPE.

ATSUMA IS JUST A SOFTIE.

zi-ip

TALKING TO YOURSELF AT A TIME LIKE THIS?
GRIN
YOU'RE AWFULLY CONFIDENT.

FLARE
FLARE
FLARE
!?
WOOSH

JUMP

FLARE
TWEEN

splat
ALRIGHT!
THUMP
IN SYNCH!

THUMP
RIGHT?
!
IT WAS A COINCIDENCE.
turn
SIZZLE
YOU'RE NO FUN.
ALL OF YOUR CAT TOYS ARE BROKEN.
ANY MORE IN STOCK?
MAYBE YOU?
I WOULDN'T BE MUCH FUN.

YOU'RE AWFULLY LOYAL TO YOUR MASTER.
YOU'RE NO DIFFERENT.

PLUS I'VE BEEN ORDERED NOT TO GET SCRATCHED.

TOUCH

ARE YOU THAT WAY TOO?

!

slap

I GUESS I DO HAVE FINER HAIR THAN YOU.
smile

he heh
STEP

ACCORDING TO THE DATA FROM THIS BATTLE...
... HE IS CLASS SSS.
WHICH MEANS...
beep
SSS

...IMMEASURABLE.
YES.
flip

NOA'S STRENGTH WILL TEMPORARILY LOWER DUE TO THE LOSS OF THE MAGATSU-HEI.
BUT THIS INFORMATION WAS WELL WORTH IT.

WAS I USEFUL TO YOU...
...GENERAL SHIKI?
THANK YOU FOR YOUR HELP...
...YANAGI.
JUST TWO GUYS AND THIS MUCH LOSS.
LADY SUMIRE...
...KEEPS VERY DANGEROUS PEOPLE AROUND HER.

EVEN I WOULD BE HARD PRESSED TO DEFEAT THEM.
YOU'RE SO MODEST.

BUT WE STILL DON'T KNOW WHAT HIS OBJECTIVE IS.

I THINK IT'S NATURAL TO THINK THAT HE IS A SPY FROM THE RESEARCH FACILITY...
...SINCE NOA TOOK POLITICAL CONTROL AFTER THE GRAND SINKER.
BUT HE SEEMED TO BE LOOKING UP INFORMATION ON NOA'S ORIGINS.
SO IT'S POSSIBLE THAT HE'S FROM A COMPLETELY DIFFERENT ORGANIZATION.

HYDE IS GOING TO MAKE HIS MOVE SOON.
WE SHOULD LEARN MORE SOON ENOUGH.

CONTINUE TO KEEP AN EYE OUT AND REPORT TO ME.
YES, SIR.

he-heh

I HOPE...

...THAT LORD HYDE WILL BE A GOOD LITTLE PAWN.

I DON'T WANT HIM TO FIND OUT THAT I PLAYED WITH HIS NEW TOY.
SO I'LL GO BACK TO WATCHING HIM.
tap
PLEASE EXCUSE ME.
tap

AND THERE'S BEEN NO REPORT SINCE THEN.
WHERE COULD SHUI BE?
HMPH
NEGLECTING YOUR ASSIGNMENT IS AGAINST ORGANIZATION RULES! AS HIS SUPERVISOR...
YOU'RE UNUSUALLY EMOTIONAL TODAY, AIKA.

IT'S LIKE YOU'RE UPSET THAT SHUI IS SO DISTRACTED.

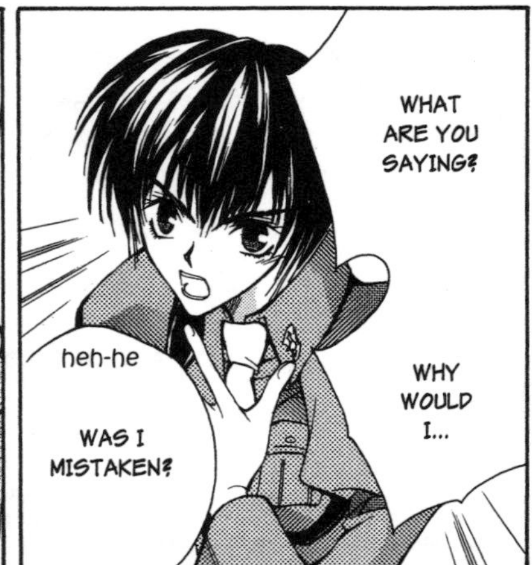
WHAT ARE YOU SAYING?
WHY WOULD I...
heh-he
WAS I MISTAKEN?

IF I WERE YOU...

...I'D BE JEALOUS.

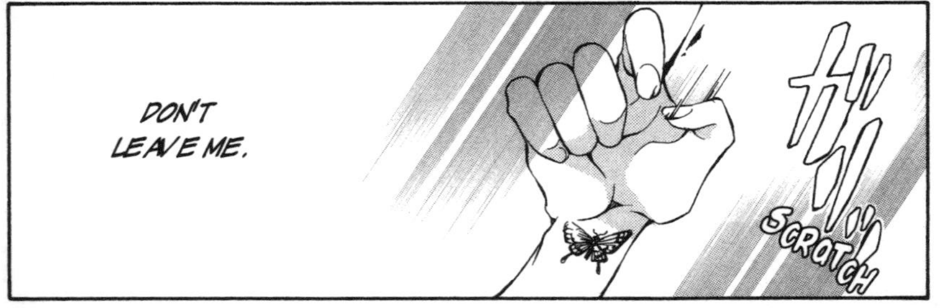
DON'T LEAVE ME.
SCRATCH

......
PLEASE.
LADY SUMIRE?
I DON'T WANT ANYONE ELSE...
...TO LEAVE MY SIDE.

I HAVEN'T TAKEN A MORNING WALK FOR A LONG TIME.

AND I EVEN GOT SOME EXERCISE ALREADY.

WELL, I DON'T THINK YOU'LL GET ALONG WITH EVERYONE HERE,
BUT ONCE YOU GET USED TO IT, NOA ISN'T A BAD PLACE TO LIVE.

THEY DO SAY HOME IS WHERE THE HEART IS.
WHY HAVEN'T YOU ASKED ME ANYTHING?

IN THIS WORLD WHERE WE DON'T EVEN KNOW IF THERE'S A FUTURE...

...I THINK IT'S SILLY TO ASK PEOPLE WHY THEY DO WHAT THEY DO.

IT'S NOT MY POLICY TO QUESTION PEOPLE,
WHO DO WHAT THEY WANT.

THEN...
...DON'T BOTHER ME.

IF YOU DON'T LIKE TO INTRUDE ON OTHERS,
THEN LEAVE ME.
IF YOU WERE JUST ANY "OTHER," THEN I WOULDN'T CARE.

BUT I TOLD YOU...

...ATSUMA.

twitch

YOU'RE LIKE A CUTE YOUNGER BROTHER TO ME.

nudge

ALL I WANT TO KNOW FROM YOU IS WHAT YOU WANT FOR BREAKFAST.

I GUESS.

DO YOU WANT TO MAKE A HOME AND FORGET YOUR MISSION?

NO WAY.
HE MIGHT BETRAY YOU TOO.
THE ONE WITH THE SAME VOICE.
GLARE

YOU HAVE TO COMPLETE YOUR MISSION.

CAN YOU SENSE IT?

THE TIME OF DESTRUCTION IS NEARLY AT HAND.

DON'T FORGET, ATSUMA.

WHY WE CAME TO THIS CITY.

AND WHY WE ENTERED THIS ORGANIZATION.

RING

TO END THE CHAOS IN THIS WORLD...
...WE HAVE TO TAKE IT BACK.
THE STOLEN SACRED SPIRIT...
...OKIKURUMI.

..NO TIME TO WASTE.

WOOOO

Volume 01 END

S
HINGO
N
ANAMI

AFTER TALK

This is my second published manga. And it's a "volume 1!"

Ever since I was a student, I was a chronic procrastinator, doing all-nighters right before tests. Since I always wait til the last minute to do anything, I don't have the personality to be a serial manga artist.

But with all of the support from various people, I have been able to publish this book.

To all my readers, to my editor, and to my private friends, thank you very much.

I'm a major penguin-freak. (If it's a baby penguin, even better.)

I would like to thank my readers who send me postcards, photos, plushies, and other penguin goodies along with fanletters. It makes me so happy. I will continue to collect penguin goodies for the rest of my life!

I will be going to the zoo to penguin-watch this year again.

DAILY LIFE

This is my friend Yunpei, who helps me put screentones on the clothes.

Boat-race betting maniac.

Mamame LOVE

We watch a lot of TV and movies together.

We have a Nausicaa, Laputa, and Princess Mononoke marathon while pasting screentones.

Not looking at screen

Princess sister!

Princess sister!

scratch, scratch

We see it so often, we memorized the lines.

In the afternoon, Yunpei rents Romeo's Blue Sky. (The first four volumes of an eight volume series.)

We watch.

When we saw the time, it was night. We rushed to the video rental store to get the rest.

beep

What are we doing?

Too old to be renting this stuff.

We watch more and cry.

And realize it's already morning.

SHOCK.

Alfred!

Oh no...

CURRENT FAD

I'm a fool for character stuff.

So I got hooked on a certain blue creature mascot.

This

When they have bonus items at the convenience store, I buy in bulk.

Yay

Both of us go.

A while ago, in order to get a white cat, I kept buying C*lpico too.

I usually drink tea, so it's hard to drink the sweet stuff. But to get the bonuses, I keep buying them.

SEE YOU IN VOLUME 2!

← I always wanted to say this phrase.

I get excited when I release a new book.

I'd love to hear comments from you.

Fanletters to: Broccoli Books
fanmail@broccolibooks.com

Shinlu sake

♥ SPECIAL THANKS to Yukie-san.

TERMINOLOGY カムイ

Grand Sinker - The second of two great earthquakes that have left Japan devastated. The southernmost islands of Kyushu and Shikoku are both completely submerged, and a good percentage of the main island Honshu is left underwater.

Atanan - Monsters that suddenly appeared after the Grand Sinker.

NOA - Stands for Noble Offensive Academy. It is a society of young men and women who have been infused with kamui in order to fight the atanan. It is backed by a government research facility that has been performing paranormal experiments on humans.

KAMUI - A term used to refer to the spirits.

EDEN - A part of the former city of Tokyo that was protected from the earthquakes by the government research facility's barrier. It is now controlled by NOA.

Tohsu - A term used to refer to the powers used by members of NOA.

I'touren - A term referring to the spirit embodied by members of NOA. For example, Lady Sumire embodies the wind i'touren.

Okikurumi - An ancient spirit and the most sacred kamui that is stolen from Atsuma's village. Its disappearance has a key role in the recent natural disasters and appearance of the atanan.

Pg. 2
Tensho - "Tensho" is Japanese and roughly translates to "Commander of the Heaven (Division)." Within NOA, Sumire holds the rank of Tensho.

Pg. 13
Kyuushu, Shikoku, Honshu - Respectively, these are the second, fourth, and first largest islands of Japan. Kyushu is the most southerly, with Shikoku just to the northeast. Just north of that is Honshu, the region most people are familiar with.

Pg. 83
Hokkaido - The second largest island of Japan located north of Honshu near Russia's eastern coastline.

Pg. 108
Ten-i, Chi-i - "Ten" is Japanese for "heaven," and "chi" is Japanese for "Earth," so the terms roughly correspond to "Heaven Officer" and "Earth Officer."

Pg. 117
Chisho - "Chisho" is Japanese and roughly translates to "Commander of the Earth (Division)." Within NOA, Hyde holds the rank of Chisho.

Pg. 150
Magatsu-hei - Japanese, it literally translates to "misfortune soldier."

Pg. 183
Nausicaa, Laputa, Princess Mononoke - *Nausicaa of the Valley of the Wind*, *Castle in the Sky* (*Laputa*), and *Princess Mononoke* are Japanese animated films by world-renowned director Hayao Miyazaki.

Romeo's Blue Sky - Japanese animated program that aired in 1995 as part of the long-running series, World Masterpiece Theater.

カムイ NOA CHAIN OF COMMAND

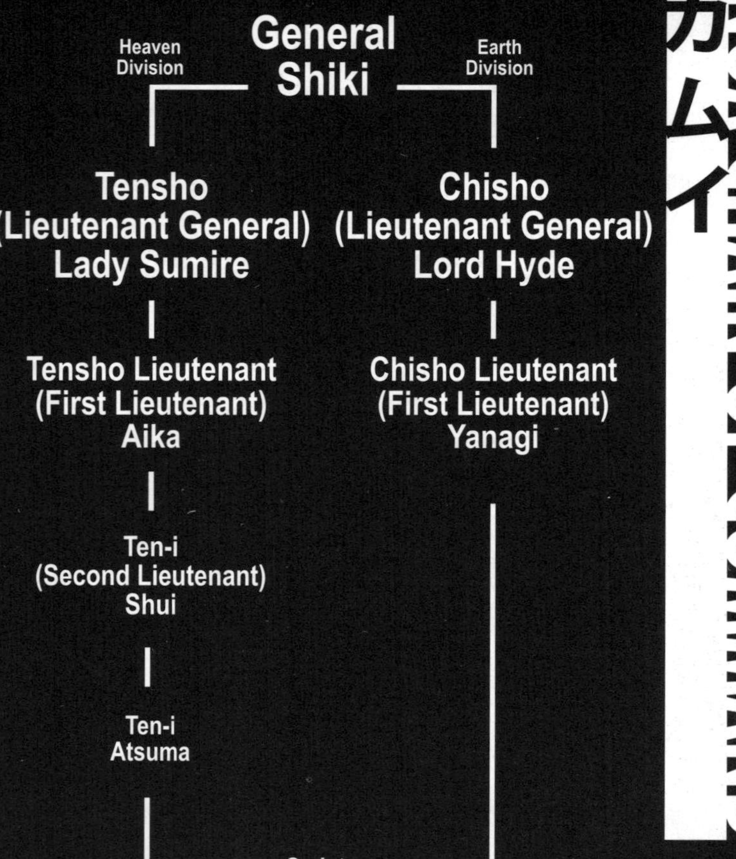

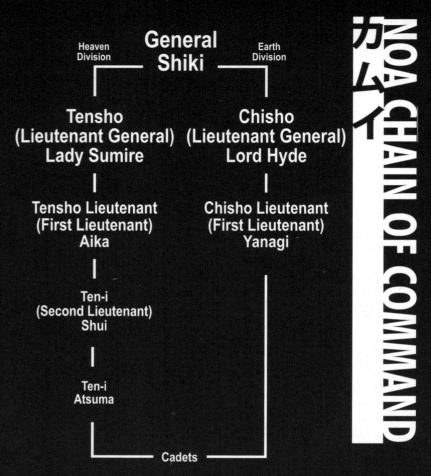

KAMUI

VOLUME 2 PREVIEW カムイ

When Atsuma defeats an atanan and saves a NOA cadet, Anzu, he gains both unwanted fame and a follower. Despite an unwillingness to respond to Anzu's admiration, Atsuma relents to taking her to NOA's annual ball.

But there are some who see Anzu as a way to strike Atsuma where he is most weak. With NOA's annual ball approaching, their plan could unleash a devastating reaction.

VOLUME 2 WILL BE GREAT! (BECAUSE I'M ON THE COVER, HEH.)
!

THUD
rip
RIGHT?
COMRADE?
HOW DO YOU LIKE...
...THE PARTY FAVOR I GAVE YOU?

SO I AM...
...THE HAPPIEST LITTLE ROCK.
DID I ASSUME WRONG?
ARE YOU SO WEAK?
YOU'RE NOT EVEN WORTH PLAYING...
What happens next!? Read more in volume 2!

by Kanan

Why settle for just one?
ギャラクシーエンジェル
Galaxy Angel™
PARTY
1
Fifteen stories featuring the five lovely Angels!
With stories by Kanan, Botan Hanayashiki, Hina., Kazuki Shu, and more!
brought to you by
BROCCOLI BOOKS
www.bro-usa.com
© 2005 BROCCOLI
Illust. by Kanan.

Leave it to Piyoko!

PLANET ANALOGUE WILL BE RICH!!

Join the celebration!

Di Gi Charat Theater - Leave it to Piyoko!, starring none other than Pyocola-sama, is coming out!

Support us, the Black Gema Gema Gang, and our mission to save Planet Analogue by buying the manga!!

Coming soon to your local bookstores!

Get Ready for Adventure!
ONLY DEJIKO AND HER FRIENDS
CAN SAVE THE GAMERS STORE!
DI GI CHARAT
THEATER
Dejiko's Adventure
TM
by Yuki Kiriga
brought to you by
BROCCOLI BOOKS
www.bro-usa.com

DI GI CHARAT™
The Original Series
© BROCCOLI • TBS
© 2005 BROCCOLI Illust. by Koge-Donbo
AVAILABLE NOW ON DVD!
Synch-Point
For more information:
www.bro-usa.com

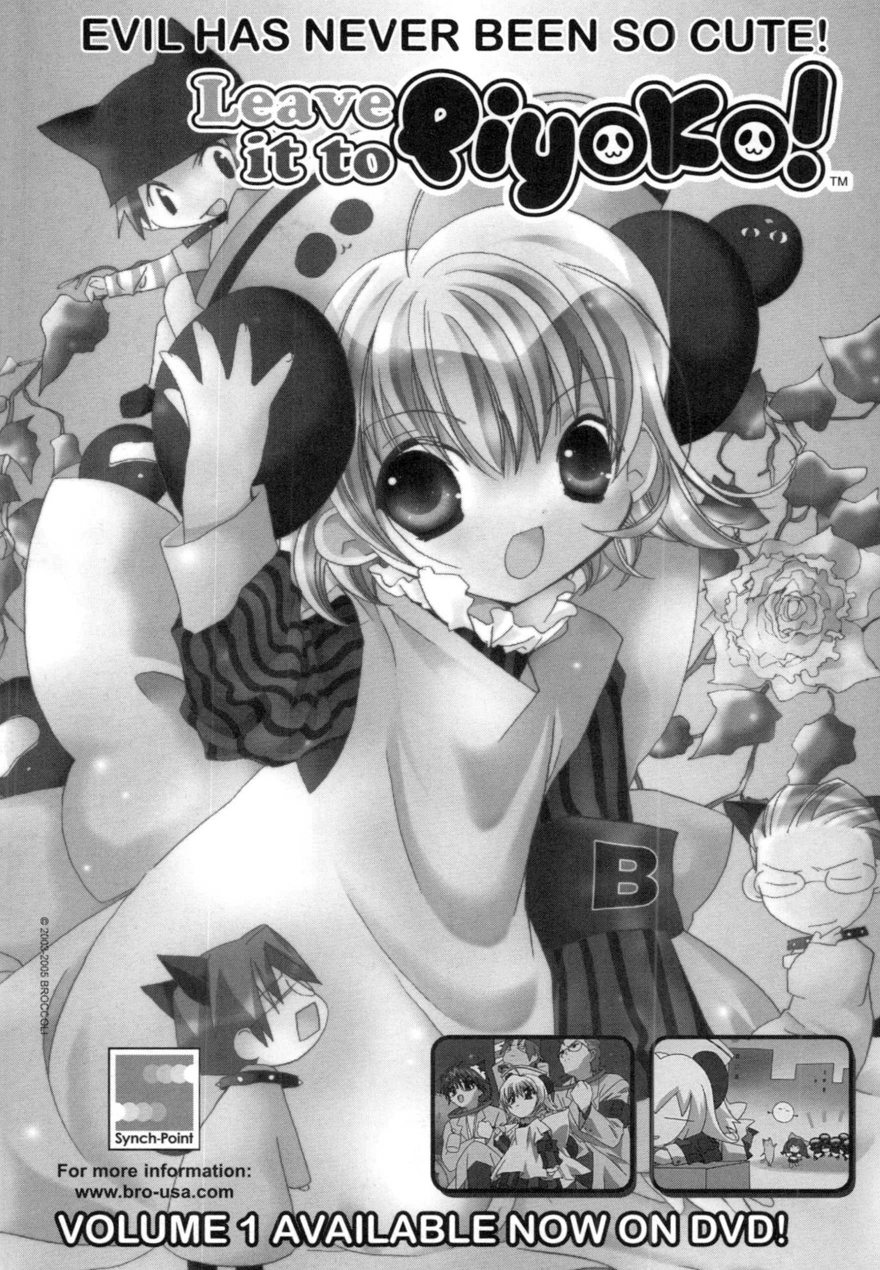
EVIL HAS NEVER BEEN SO CUTE!
Leave it to Piyoko!™
B
© 2003-2005 BROCCOLI
Synch-Point
For more information:
www.bro-usa.com
VOLUME 1 AVAILABLE NOW ON DVD!

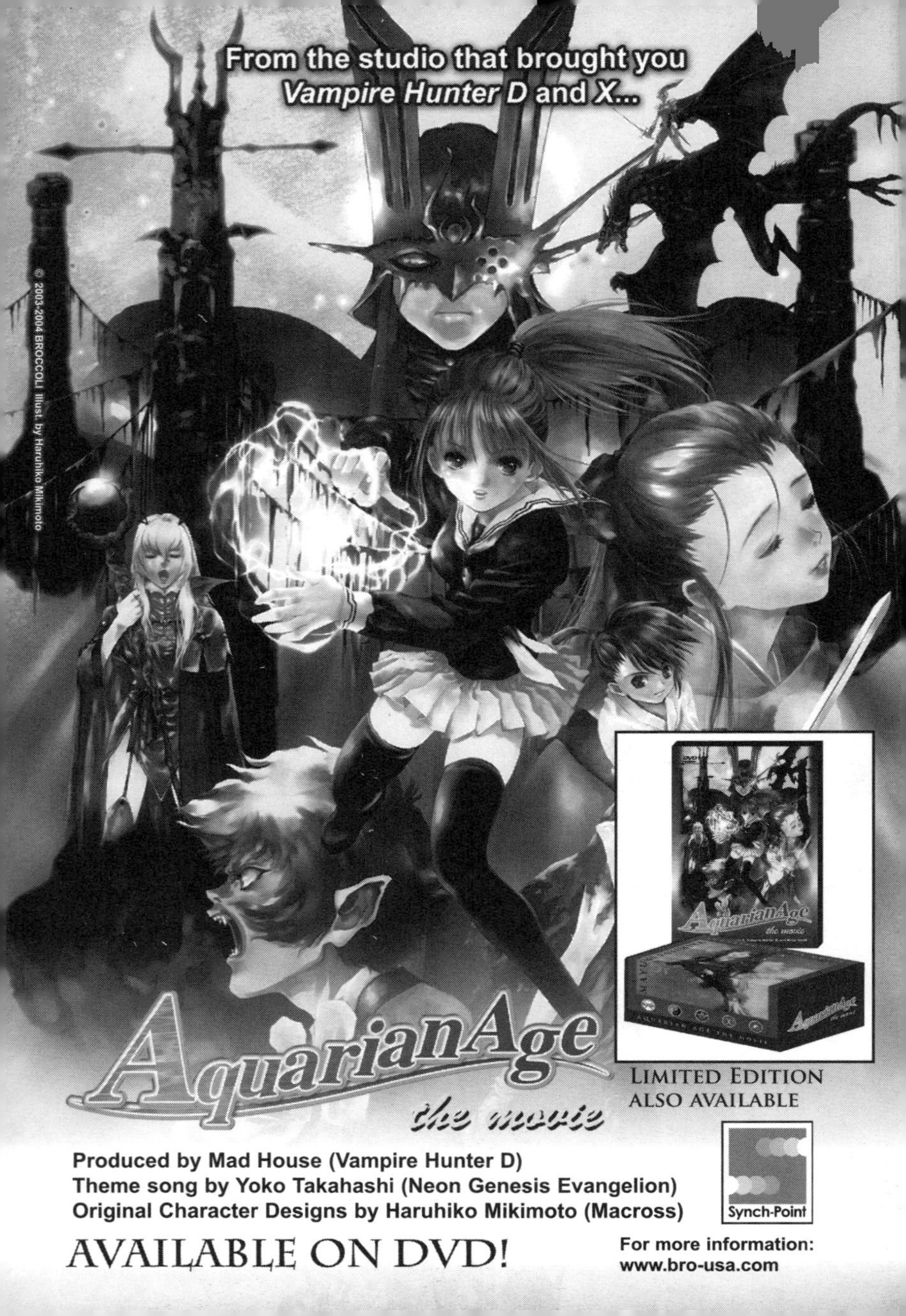

From the studio that brought you *Fushigi Yûgi* and *Yu Yu Hakusho*

I'm Gonna Be An Angel!

TENSHI NI NARUMON

Angels. Monsters. And Mystery Men. Oh my!

Brought to you by

NOW AVAILABLE ON DVD

www.bro-usa.com

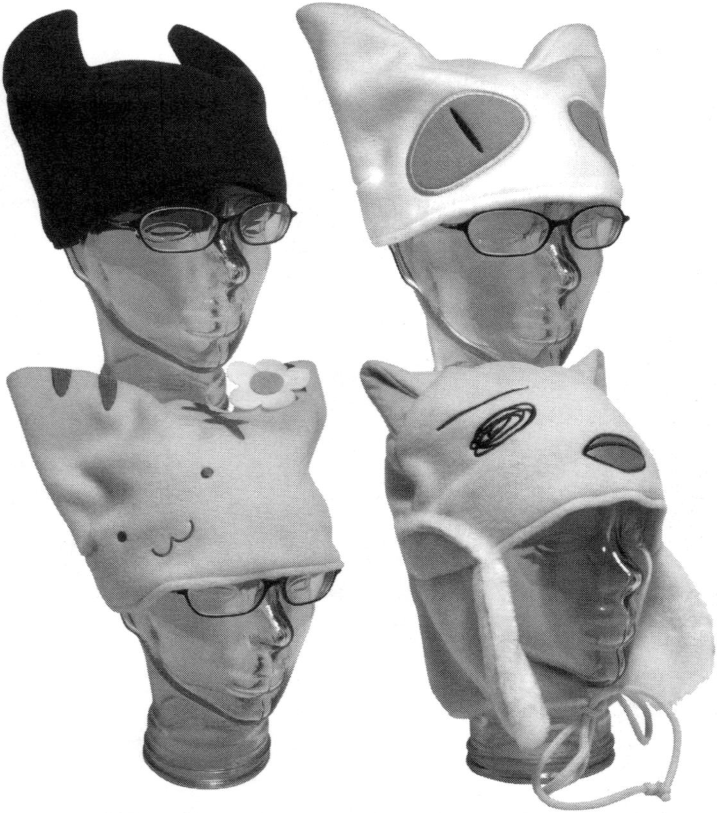

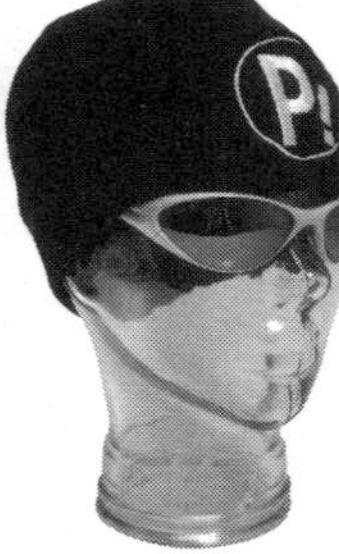

STOP!
YOU'RE READING THE WRONG WAY!

This is the end of the book! In Japan, manga is generally read from right to left. All reading starts on the upper right corner, and ends on the lower left. American comics are generally read from left to right, starting on the upper left of each page. In order to preserve the true nature of the work, we printed this book in a right to left fashion. Those who are unfamiliar with manga may find this confusing at first, but once you start getting into the story, you will wonder how you ever read manga any other way!

KA

THIS QUESTIONNAIRE IS REDEEMABLE FOR:

KAMUI Volume 1 Dust Jacket

Broccoli Books Questionnaire

Fill out and return to Broccoli Books to receive your corresponding dust jacket!*

PLEASE MAIL THE COMPLETE FORM, ALONG WITH UNUSED UNITED STATES POSTAGE STAMPS WORTH $1.50 ENCLOSED IN THE ENVELOPE TO:**

Broccoli International
Attn: Broccoli Books Dust Jacket Committee
P.O. Box 66078
Los Angeles, CA 90066

(Please write legibly)

Name: ______________________________

Address: ______________________________

City, State, Zip: ______________________________

E-mail: ______________________________

Gender: ☐ Male ☐ Female **Age:** ________

(If you are under 13 years old, parental consent is required)

Parent/Guardian signature: ______________________________

Occupation: ______________________________

Where did you hear about this title?

☐ Magazine (Please specify): ______________________________

☐ Flyer from: a store convention club other: ______________________________

☐ Website (Please specify): ______________________________

☐ At a store (Please specify): ______________________________

☐ Word of Mouth

☐ Other (Please specify): ______________________________

Where was this title purchased? (If known)

____

Why did you buy this title?

____

____

____

CUT ALONG HERE

How would you rate the following features of this manga?

	Excellent	Good	Satisfactory	Poor
Translation	☐	☐	☐	☐
Art quality	☐	☐	☐	☐
Cover	☐	☐	☐	☐
Extra/Bonus Material	☐	☐	☐	☐

What would you like to see improved in Broccoli Books manga?

____

Would you recommend this manga to someone else? ☐ Yes ☐ No

What related products would you be interested in?

☐ Posters ☐ Apparel Other: ______________________________

Which magazines do you read on a regular basis?

____

What manga titles would you like to see in English?

____

Favorite manga titles: ______________________________

Favorite manga artists: ______________________________

What race/ethnicity do you consider yourself? (Please check one)

☐ Asian/Pacific Islander ☐ Native American/Alaskan Native
☐ Black/African American ☐ White/Caucasian
☐ Hispanic/Latino ☐ Other: ______________________________

Final comments about this manga:

____

____

____

Thank you!

* While supplies last.
** For Canada residents, please send an international money order of $3.00 made out to "Broccoli International."

All information provided will be used for internal purposes only. We will not sell or otherwise divulge any of the information.

Requests not in compliance with all terms of this form will not be acknowledged or returned. All submissions are subject to verification and become the property of Broccoli International USA. Fraudulent submission, including use of multiple addresses or P.O. boxes to obtain additional Broccoli International USA information or offers may result in prosecution. Broccoli International USA reserves the right to withdraw or modify any terms of this form. Void where prohibited, taxed, or restricted by law. Broccoli International USA will not be liable for lost, misdirected, mutilated, illegible, incomplete, or postage-due mail. Dust jacket offer is only available to residents of the United States and Canada. For updates to the rules and regulations, please see www.broccolibooks.com.

CUT ALONG HERE